STEM Jobs
in Music

Shirley Duke

rourkeeducationalmedia.com

Before Reading:

Building Academic Vocabulary and Background Knowledge

Before reading a book, it is important to tap into what your child or students already know about the topic. This will help them develop their vocabulary, increase their reading comprehension, and make connections across the curriculum.

1. *Look at the cover of the book. What will this book be about?*
2. *What do you already know about the topic?*
3. *Let's study the Table of Contents. What will you learn about in the book's chapters?*
4. *What would you like to learn about this topic? Do you think you might learn about it from this book? Why or why not?*
5. *Use a reading journal to write about your knowledge of this topic. Record what you already know about the topic and what you hope to learn about the topic.*
6. *Read the book.*
7. *In your reading journal, record what you learned about the topic and your response to the book.*
8. *After reading the book complete the activities below.*

Content Area Vocabulary
Read the list. What do these words mean?

acoustic
algorithms
audio
auditory
baffles
digital
electromagnetic
enhance
mixed
neuroscientists
technicians
scan
session
sound waves

After Reading:

Comprehension and Extension Activity

After reading the book, work on the following questions with your child or students in order to check their level of reading comprehension and content mastery.

1. *Describe the role of STEM in the music industry. (Summarize)*
2. *Why might an artist use software to digitally alter the sound of his or her voice? (Infer)*
3. *What skills would you need to become a music therapist? (Text to self connection)*
4. *Describe how algorithms recommend new music suggestions. (Summarize)*
5. *Describe how sound acts in an open space compared to a closed room. (Visualize)*

Extension Activity

Create a Venn diagram comparing and contrasting an acoustic guitar with an electric guitar. How are the instruments similar? How are they different?

Table of Contents

What Is STEM?

A sound engineer adjusts the controls on a soundboard. A sound designer creates a new effects tool. A music therapist helps someone recover after a stroke.

These people all have jobs in music. Yet, each one is in a STEM field. STEM means science, technology, engineering, and mathematics. Music is using sound to express emotions through combined notes in a pleasing way. It's also a big part of STEM jobs. Many music jobs involve STEM subjects.

STEM jobs relate to many fields. In music, the jobs range from developing new effects to recording performances. STEM jobs meet needs people have. It then allows them to work in a field they enjoy. Talent in music helps, but not every STEM music job requires great musical talent. A STEM education can prepare you to work in the exciting field of music.

What does STEM stand for?
Science
Technology
Engineering
Mathematics

Creating Great Sound

The latest album from your favorite band just came out. You hit play and you hear… perfection! You can thank the sound engineers for a first class listening experience. They make the recording just right. What would you think if you heard muffled voices? Too loud drums? Off key notes? The sound engineer balances the music so you hear the song the way you are meant to.

Technology and creativity come together when an audio engineer mixes a recording.

Artists have a vision for the sound they want. They discuss their plans with the **audio** team. They decide how to record the music, what equipment to use, and what effects to apply. The sounds are **mixed** to make the recording come together.

The sounds you hear in recorded or broadcast music have been controlled and adjusted by people working in this field. They use layers of sound to make movies, songs, and videos come alive.

STEM in Action!

Listen to one of your favorite songs. Use a stereo or computer that lets you adjust the sound.

Slowly turn the bass up. Then turn it down. What change did you notice in the way the song sounded?

Return the bass to the center position. Now adjust the treble. Do the same for the balance. How did these affect the sound? In what position does the song sound its best?

Sound **technicians** work to develop new equipment and improve existing technology. Music companies will add to and upgrade old systems.

Sound and recording equipment is used in many companies outside of the music industry as well. Many companies are using video conferences to cut costs and improve communication. Sound technicians develop the right tools for these situations.

Real STEM Job: *Sound Technician*

Sound technicians run the equipment to record, mix, and reproduce music. They do this for music, voices, and sound effects. They work with the artist and producer to bring a complete vision to the recording.

Technicians use high-tech **digital** tools to make changes to the original performance. The recording will be played on television, radios, and on the albums fans purchase. Sound technicians make sure that these recordings are perfect.

This job requires strong computer skills and technical knowledge. It takes an understanding of sound and its equipment. If you like on-the-job training and creating great sound, this might be a career for you.

Mixing consoles give technicians great control over the quality of a sound.

Sound in Space

Depending on where you are, sound has different qualities. In your classroom, it is easy to hear the teacher talking to your class. But if you are outside on a windy day, it may be difficult to hear a friend calling for you across the yard. If you have ever been in a large, empty auditorium, you may have heard your voice echo.

Acoustic engineers understand how sound moves in different spaces.

Acoustics and noise control are more complex matters than they might appear. The ceiling plays an important role in noise control. Acoustic engineers are familiar with the need for acoustical ceilings.

Sound is a form of energy. When you pluck a guitar string, it vibrates back and forth. These vibrations form **sound waves**, which can travel through air, water, and even solid materials.

STEM in Action!

Get out your favorite song. Listen to it through portable speakers. Take your device outside and listen again. Now, play it on your headphones. Try it again on a car stereo.

Compare the sound in each situation. Did you notice any differences?

The type of equipment you use to play music can change the quality of the sound. So can the size of the room you are in. Sound bounces off walls and into your ears. Where is the best place you can find to listen to music?

Theaters are designed to spread sound evenly, knowing that actors may perform without the aid of microphones.

When sound waves hit a hard surface they are reflected back. Acoustic engineers study how sound travels in different spaces. They use this knowledge to design theaters, auditoriums, and other spaces in which sound is important. They create unique experiences for audiences.

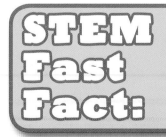

STEM Fast Fact: Acoustic engineers design soundproof rooms that absorb sound.

Real STEM Job: *Acoustic Engineer*

In auditoriums and performance spaces, engineers will add devices like baffles to improve sound. Some acoustic engineers specialize in building design. They work with architects from the start to create a space that will enhance sound.

Sometimes, acoustic engineers focus on noise control. They design barriers to keep sound from disturbing neighbors.

Acoustic engineers know how sound moves. They study physics, engineering, and math. Next time you're in a theater or concert hall, see if you can find how an acoustic engineer improved your listening experience.

Sound baffles may be used when constructing a sound-proof room.

Large open auditoriums allow music to pleasantly reverberate off the walls.

Better with Music

Music has an incredible ability to change a person's mood. Music therapy helps people with physical, emotional, or learning needs. Research shows that music therapy helps people improve their physical condition. It supports their emotions. They can more easily express their feelings and communicate better.

Listening to music can help reduce pain up to 25 percent in some people and helps them feel more in control of long-term pain.

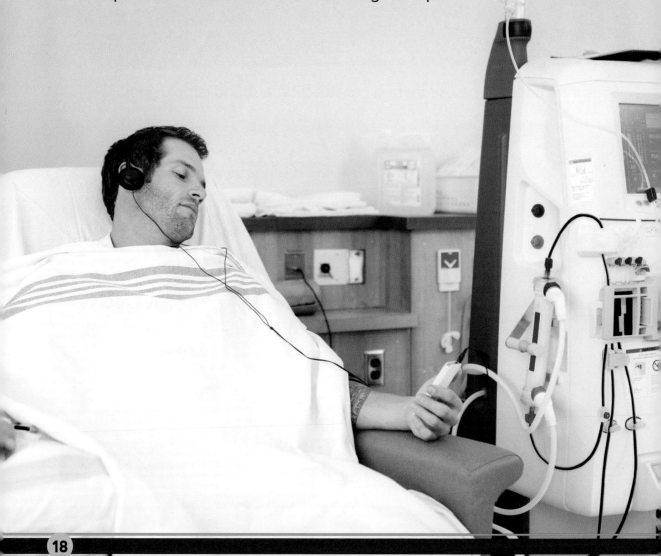

Music therapy gives patients a new way to communicate. Learning music may improve memory, muscle movement, and social skills.

Every patient needing music therapy is different. Therapists aid adults and children with mental illness, brain injuries, delays in development, disabilities, physical problems, and speech and hearing problems.

Music therapy has been used to treat people suffering from dementia, asthma, autism, and Parkinson's. It may be used to reduce pain, improve sleep, control weight, and improve communication abilities.

STEM in Action!

Grab your music collection or flip through the dial on a radio. Pick different kinds of music to listen to.

Start with a pop song. Close your eyes and listen to the entire song. How does the song make you feel? Happy? Excited? Energetic?

Now try a classical song. How do you feel now? Calm? Relaxed? Bored?

Keep listening to different types of music and decide how each type makes you feel. Keep a record of all the songs, their genres, and the feelings they created. Try country, rock, jazz, hip-hop, and metal.

If you had a friend who was feeling sad, what song would you recommend for them?

A music therapy **session** may be different for each patient. It depends on the patient's needs, abilities, and musical tastes. A patient may listen to popular songs or practice deep breathing while listening to relaxing music. Other therapies include singing, playing instruments, writing song lyrics, dancing to music, or discussing how songs made them feel.

Music therapists often work in a team of medical workers. Music therapy is just one part of a patient's treatment. They are often prescribed medications and other therapies.

Research has shown music therapy to be helpful for people with Alzheimer's and dementia.

Real STEM Job: *Music Therapist*

Music therapy helps people with problems and disabilities. It combines music with therapy. This field is growing. It offers a wide variety of jobs.

Music therapists identify the needs of patients. Then they design a treatment plan. This may include creating, singing, moving, or listening to music. Music therapy improves peoples' abilities physically. It allows them to transfer those skills to other parts of their lives.

Music therapists work in nursing homes, prisons, hospitals, rehab centers, day care centers, schools, and in private practice. Music therapists study music and science. This job requires a degree and certification in music therapy.

Music and the Brain

Music therapists know how music can have an effect on a patient's well-being. But how does music actually affect a person's brain? That is a question for **neuroscientists**, or scientists who study the brain.

Doctors collect scans of different slices of the brain using an fMRI machine.

In order to study how music affects the brain, volunteers listen to music while scientists **scan** their brains. The pictures from the scans let scientists know what areas of the brain were active. One part that understands language lights up. Another lights up that understands melody. Another part lights up because the song makes the listener feel good. This information helps the scientists understand how we learn, remember, and feel emotions.

STEM in Action!

The brain is responsible for many things. It is the body's control center. It senses the world around us, controls the body's muscles, and remembers past experiences.

Test how well your brain's memory works. Pick a random phone number out of the telephone book. Study the phone number for 5 minutes. Then test yourself. Do you remember the whole thing? If not, study the number some more until you have it memorized.

Test yourself again in 5 minutes. Can you remember it 20 minutes later? How about 2 hours later? How about the next day?

Did you have trouble remembering the phone number? Why do you think that it was so difficult to remember those numbers? What does this say about short-term and long-term memory?

Scientists also study the brains of music performers. For musicians, even more parts of the brain are active when listening to music. When different areas of the brain light up on scans, scientists can learn how the brain makes connections.

Scientists analyze brain scans to understand how the brain works.

Real STEM Job: *Auditory Neuroscientist*

Scientists who specialize in studying music and the brain are **auditory** neuroscientists. They ask questions about how the brain works. Then they design experiments, run tests, and observe volunteers as they listen to or create music.

Their research can help scientists better understand the brain. Sometimes their research can help develop new treatments for people who are deaf.

Auditory neuroscientists have training in the sciences and technology. They study the brain, the body, psychology, music, and computers.

Scientists can measure brain activity by attaching electrodes to the scalp and face. The electrodes record brain activity and send the information to the computer.

Recommendation Engine

After buying the latest hit album online, you get an email suggesting other artists you might want to listen to. Some of the artists you like, some you don't, and some are brand new to you. How did your computer figure out what new music to suggest?

Many websites will suggest the newest, most popular music that best matches your previous buying history.

Many websites that sell music use computer calculations called **algorithms**. These calculations find music similar to what you have already listened to. The computer looks at what you like and compares it to what people with similar tastes also like. It suggests other artists in the same genre. It suggests the most popular artists that fit your tastes.

These suggestions help music fans discover new music. They also help websites sell more music to their customers. By improving their algorithm, a website can offer better suggestions and improve sales.

STEM in Action!

Say you are trying to recommend music for a listener on an online radio station. After each song, the listener rates it as +1 if they liked it or -1 if they did not. Below is a list of the listener's ratings for 15 songs in a few different genres.

Country	-1	Hip-hop	+1
Rock	-1	Rock	+1
Hip-hop	+1	Country	-1
Hip-hop	-1	Rock	+1
Rock	+1	Pop	+1
Pop	+1	Hip-hop	+1
Pop	+1	Rock	-1
Rock	-1		

What is the listener's favorite genre? Find their preference by adding the ratings.

Country	-1 + -1 = -2
Rock	-1 + 1 + -1 + 1 + 1 + -1 = 0
Hop-hip	1 + -1 + 1 + 1 = 2
Pop	1 + 1 + 1 = 3

This listener rated pop music the highest.

Do you think 15 songs are enough to give a good recommendation? Would it have helped to know which artists or songs the listener had rated? What information would you ask to get better recommendations?

Real STEM Job: *Data Scientist*

Recommending new music is all about data. The more information available, the better the recommendations can get. Data scientists study the data they have and try to improve their recommendations. They make improvements to their algorithm.

They may add new ratings options for users to tell them what they like. Or they may be able to assign qualities to the music the listener is choosing. They can then find songs with similar melodies, lyrics, or rhythms. However they do it, data scientists make sense of very large amounts of data to give personal recommendations.

Data scientists are skilled at computers and mathematics. If you're skilled at math and enjoy music, this may be the job for you.

Tools for Music

Creating music is an art. But technology plays an important role in producing, performing, and listening to music.

Instruments like electric guitars and keyboards help musicians create their music. A guitar player will select pickups, effects pedals, and amplifiers to get the right tone for the music. Many companies have experts in music and electronics to create the unique devices that musicians use.

Guitar effects pedals may create distortion, modulation, feedback, and other effects.

Technology helps vocal performers as well. Computer software can be used to create unique effects on a singer's voice. Or it can simply alter the singer's pitch so that any mistakes are corrected. This technology is often used in recording. However, some performers even use it during live performances.

STEM in Action!

Digital effects are great at changing the sound of music. Still, some tools do not require special technology to alter sound.

Start by covering your mouth with your hand. Now, sing into your hand. What effect did this have on your voice?

Try this experiment again by singing into an empty paper towel roll, a comb covered with wax paper, and an electric fan. How did each of these things change the sound of your voice?

Find other objects or create your own device to alter your voice. You may discover a great new effect.

Technology has also changed the way that music fans experience their favorite music. At first, music lovers bought their favorite albums on records. Then new technology brought their music to cassettes and CDs. Now, music is sold digitally. Fans listen on MP3 players, smartphones, and computers.

STEM Spotlight Inventing the Electric Guitar

The electric guitar is one of the most important modern instruments. Guitar makers, engineers, and musicians had been looking for a way to make their guitars louder for years. They experimented with larger guitar bodies, metal bodies, and electricity.

In the 1930s, inventors developed an **electromagnetic** pickup that amplified guitar strings' vibration. When the guitar is plugged into an amplifier, the vibrations are turned into sound. With this new, louder, bolder instrument, popular music changed forever.

A cast aluminum guitar, developed in 1931, is the model for the technology used in most electric guitars today.

T-Bone Walker (1910–1975) was one of the first popular guitarists to use an amplified guitar, developing his sound into the classic blues we know today.

The solid body Gibson guitar is one of the world's most popular electric guitars.

The Future in Music

More changes are sure to come as the music industry grows. Technology will continue to develop new ways of bringing music to listeners. Jobs in music provide ways to create and perform in a field that requires talent.

A STEM education will open up opportunities in this industry. Music lovers with the skills to create, study, and analyze will bring fantastic new changes to music.

STEM Job Fact Sheets

Sound Technician

Important Skills: Speaking, Active Listening, Critical Thinking, Reading Comprehension, Monitoring Performance

Important Knowledge: Computers, Electronics, Communications, Media, Customer Service, Engineering, Technology, Fine Arts

College Major: Communications Technology, Music Technology, Recording Arts Technology

Median Salary: $54,030

Acoustic Engineer

Important Skills: Active Listening, Critical Thinking, Speaking, Reading Comprehension, Judgment, Decision Making

Important Knowledge: Design, Construction, Engineering, Science, Technology, Mathematics

College Major: Mechanical Engineering, Electrical Engineering, Mathematics, Physics

Median Salary: $83,000

Music Therapist

Important Skills: Communication, Critical Thinking, Social Perceptiveness, Patience

Important Knowledge: Psychology, Counseling, Medicine, Music

College Major: Psychology, Therapeutic Recreation

Median Salary: $39,410

Auditory Neuroscientist

Important Skills: Science, Critical Thinking, Reading Comprehension, Speaking, Complex Problem-Solving

Important Knowledge: Biology, English Language, Mathematics, Medicine, Chemistry

College Major: Anatomy, Biochemistry, Neuroscience, Psychology, Cognitive Science

Median Salary: $86,710

Data Scientist

Important Skills: Complex Problem-Solving, Critical Thinking, Systems Analysis, Systems Evaluation, Decision Making

Important Knowledge: Computers, Mathematics, English Language, Communications

College Major: Computer Science, Statistics, Information Systems

Median Salary: $117,500

Electrical Engineering Technician

Important Skills: Critical Thinking, Complex Problem-Solving, Reading Comprehension, Operation Monitoring, Active Listening

Important Knowledge: Computers, Electronics, Mathematics, English Language, Production, Processing, Mechanical Engineering

College Major: Computer Engineering Technology, Electrical Engineering, Computer Technology, Integrated Circuit Design

Median Salary: $56,690

Glossary

acoustic (uh-KOO-stik): related to hearing or sound

algorithms (al-guh-RITH-uhms): step-by-step procedure for a computer to perform calculations

audio (AW-dee-oh): having to do with sound

auditory (aw-DUH-tor-ee): related to hearing

baffles (BAF-uhls): objects that absorb sound

digital (DIJ-i-tuhl): recording information or data in a number form for use on computers and devices

electromagnetic (i-lek-troh-MAG-nit-ik): a magnet that forms when electricity flows through a wire coil

enhance (en-HANS): to improve

mixed (MIKST): using an electronic device to combine audio signals into one sound, usually in music

neuroscientists (noor-oh-SYE-uhn-tists): scientists who study the brain

technicians (tek-NISH-uhns): people who work with specialized equipment or do practical work in a certain field

scan (skan): to examine part of the human body

session (SESH-uhn): a time period for a meeting or training

sound waves (SOUND wayvs): waves that transmit sound through a material due to a sound vibration

Index

Show What You Know

1. How does STEM apply to the music industry?
2. What materials can sound waves travel through?
3. What STEM job requires knowledge of physics?
4. Why does the author provide an activity in which the reader adjusts levels on a stereo?
5. How does data help improve recommendations?

Websites to Visit

www.kids.usa.gov/music

www.school.familyeducation.com/child-based-learning/careers/38499.html

www.classicsforkids.com/interviews

About the Author

Shirley Duke is the author of many science books for children. She taught science for many years. Her favorite music is classical and she played the piano and alto sax for ten years at school. She still enjoys music but loves writing about it.

Meet The Author!
www.meetREMauthors.com

www.rourkeeducationalmedia.com

PHOTO CREDITS: Cover © Imageegami, Christian Gasner, Silvia Jansen; Title Page © sandsun; page 4 © Kzenon; page 5 © gavmac; page 6 © Chris Schmidt; page 7, 22 © bikeriderlondon; page 8 © Michael Krakowiak; page 9 © Andriy Popov, Pekka Jaakkola; page 10 © Arne Thaysen; page 11 © Paul Vasarhelyi; page 12 © Gleb Semenov; page 13 © marcart, Petrovich9; page 14 © ambrits, Vartanov Anatoly; page 15 © adventtr; page 16 © Juanmonino; page 17 © alacatr; page 17 © willyseto; page 18 © Tyler Olson; page 19 © Miriam Doerr; page 20 © Juergen Faelchie; page 21 © goodluz; page 23 © Cathy Yeulet, energyy; page 24 © Yulia Koltyrina; page 25 © alvarez; page 26 © Justin Horrcoks; page 27 © stanley45; page 28 © Image Point Fr; page 29 © Latsalomao; page 30 © Scott Smith; page 31 © Mutlu Kurbas; page 32 © Сергей Тряпицын; page 35 © bee_photobee; page 36 © jordache; page 37 © archives; page 38 © Sinan Isakovic; page 39 © pixdeluxe; page 40 © Heinrich Klaffs/Wikipedia; page 41 © Paola Cipriani, Rapid Eye; page 42 © Oktay Ortakcioglu; page 43 © Chris Schmidt

Edited by: Jill Sherman

Cover and Interior design by: Renee Brady

Library of Congress PCN Data

STEM Jobs in Music / Shirley Duke
(STEM Jobs You'll Love)
ISBN 978-1-62717-699-6 (hard cover)
ISBN 978-1-62717-821-1 (soft cover)
ISBN 978-1-62717-935-5 (e-Book)
Library of Congress Control Number: 2014935492
Printed in the United States of America, North Mankato, Minnesota

Also Available as: